D0191655

Acknowledgements

The authors would like to recognize the contributions of
Paul Katz, Jason Heimberg, Steve Harwood,
Eric Immerman, Todd DeHart and Jon Stokes.
Thanks also to Robert Kempe and Dave Zuckerman
and to Tom Schirtz for his grand design.

To our mothers, we apologize again.
This time, more than ever.

WOULD YOU RATHER...?

The
Dirty
Version

Over 700 *Devilishly Demented Dilemmas* to Ponder

Justin Heimberg & David Gomberg

Published by Seven Footer Press
247 West 30th St., 2nd Fl.
New York, NY 10001
10 9 8 7 6 5
Printed in the United States of America

Would You Rather...?® is a registered trademark used under license from
Spin Master Ltd.

Design by Thomas Schirtz

ISBN 978-1-934734-17-9

www.sevenfooterpress.com

Table of Contents

How to Use This Book

Sit around with a bunch of friends and read a question out loud. Discuss the advantages and drawbacks of each option before making a choice. Stretch, twist, and otherwise abuse your imagination to think of the multitude of ways the choice could affect you. The question is merely a springboard for your conversation.

Everybody must choose. As the Deity proclaims, YOU MUST CHOOSE! Once everyone has chosen, move on to the next question. It's that simple.

If you receive a question directed at females, and you are a male (or vice-versa), you can do one of several things: a) move on to another question, b) answer the question anyway, or c) freak out.

On occasion, we have provided some "things to consider" when making your decisions, but do not restrict yourself to those subjects when debating. There are no limits with this book, so go ahead and get down and dirty. Say whatever is on your mind no matter how repugnant and nasty. There are few forums where one gets to express their deviant and warped side, so let loose.

Introduction

When we set out writing the original *Would You Rather...?* book, nearly fifteen years ago, bright-eyed, bushy-tailed—weight of the world having yet to quash our spirits—we aimed high. We saw the socially interactive book as a tool to facilitate philosophical inquiry, flex critical thinking, and foster community in an age of isolation. Our handiwork was a modern day Socratic Dialogue, every sentence a launching pad for the reader's imagination along with the requisite ensuing discussion and debate.

And then we realized that everybody liked the dirty stuff.

The questions that proposed having seventeen testicles versus one the size of a cantaloupe, the magnetic scrotums, images of birch beer ejaculate, depictions of fire-hose power vaginal orgasms, and so forth. The word count for "balls" jumped in each book from ten to twenty to fifty to a hundred. The Socratic Dialogues danced dangerously with Sophomoric Dialogues. The lowbrow dipped so low, it became a mustache.

And then one day, lying in our bunkbeds, sunken and ashamed, a thought crawled into our collective head: Are the two mutually exclusive? Can't the gross, sexual, and silly be woven together with the creative, intelligent, and philosophical? Does it not require mental energy to envision having your genitals on the top of your head vs. the bottom of your foot? Does it not challenge the imagination to discuss the advantages and drawbacks of having breast implants full of loose change? Or is this all rationalization to justify men in their mid-thirties still writing fart jokes? That, of course, is a question that only God can answer. We await his judgment with patience and humility. Until then, enjoy the rotten fruits of our labor. ☺

CHAPTER ONE

Who'd You Rather...?

When selecting a sexual partner, one must consider chemistry. (For example, choosing between Megan Fox covered in sulfuric acid or a helium-filled Barbara Walters.) The following quandaries propose partners from the sublime to the surreal, from famous celebrities to infamous oddities, from the "Oh yeah!" to the "Oh-bese!" Be certain, Dear Reader, that you conduct yourself with the utmost decorum when discussing such matters. Anything else would be... uncivilized.

Would you rather...

have sex with Katie Couric *OR* Natalie Portman if she gained 100 pounds?

Heidi Montag *OR* Susan Boyle if you had to then listen to each of them sing for six hours straight?

J.Lo *OR* Ashley Olsen if they exchanged asses?

Things to consider: Could Olsen support J.Lo's ass without toppling over?

YOU MUST CHOOSE!

Would you rather...

have sex with Brad Pitt if he gained 150 pounds *OR*

Jeff Foxworthy?

Spencer Pratt *OR* George Clooney if they exchanged personalities?

Mini-Me (Verne Troyer) *OR* Shaquille O'Neal?

Things to consider: being spun around like a basketball, rectal prolapse

YOU MUST CHOOSE!

Would you rather...

take it from Kelly Osbourne wearing a 3-inch strap-on

OR

from Scarlett Johansson wearing a 10-inch strap-on?

Would you rather...

have sex with Kim Kardashian

OR

a three-way with Kourtney and Khloe?

YOU MUST CHOOSE!

Would you rather...

have a girlfriend who will only give you oral sex if you do the "Vrrroooom! Here comes the airplane!" thing with your penis

OR

a girlfriend who automatically shifts into a Bill Cosby impression during all sexual activity?

YOU MUST CHOOSE!

5

By the Numbers

Would you rather...

get a hand job from a perfect 10 *OR* have sex with a 6?

a foot job from an 8 *OR* anal sex with a 5?

a knee job from a 2 *OR* brunch with a 4?

Would you rather...

have sex with a perfect 10 but get herpes

OR

have sex with a 2 and get a $10 coupon to Long John Silver's?

YOU MUST CHOOSE!

Would you rather...

have sex with Shakira *OR* Jessica Alba?

Carrie Underwood *OR* Jenna Jameson?

Angelina Jolie with the arms of a gorilla and the legs of an elephant *OR* Joy Behar?

Would you rather...

have sex with Orlando Bloom *OR* Tom Brady?

Daughtry *OR* David Archuleta?

Robert Pattinson in character as Edward Cullen *OR* Pattinson out of character?

YOU MUST CHOOSE!

It's All Relative

Would you rather...

for thirty seconds, make out with your mom

OR

with a hot curling iron?

Would you rather...

get a lap dance from your grandma

OR

give a lap dance to your grandma?

Things to consider: physical injury, psychological injury

YOU MUST CHOOSE!

Would you rather...

have the offensive line of the Nebraska Cornhuskers run the train on you

OR

on your mom?

Things to consider: lineman's average weight of 310 pounds; how much do you love your mom?

YOU MUST CHOOSE!

Date, Marry, Screw:

Which of the three would you date, which would you marry, and which would you screw?

Tin Man, Scarecrow, Cowardly Lion

Things to consider: giving your heart to the Tin Man, fucking your brains out with the Scarecrow, the Cowardly Lion = Gay?

Jennifer Aniston, Courtney Cox, Megatron

Things to consider: Aniston's legs, Cox's eyes, Megatron's desire for world domination and utter annihilation of the Autobots

YOU MUST CHOOSE!

Would you rather...

give the person on your left a massage and "happy ending"

OR

give the person on your right a thorough prostate exam?

Would you rather...

tongue-kiss the person to your left

OR

mildly grope the breast (outside the clothing) of the person on your right?

Things to consider: Make it happen.

YOU MUST CHOOSE!

The Name Game

Would you rather...

have sex with Megan Fox while she is possessed by Redd Foxx

OR

Jessica Simpson while she is possessed by Homer Simpson?

Would you... have sex with Tyne Daly, daily

to have sex with Keira Knightley, nightly?

YOU MUST CHOOSE!

Would you... get urinated on by Chuck Berry to bang Halle Berry?

Would you rather...

have sex with a living Chuck Berry

OR

a dead Halle Berry?

Things to consider: How many of you just asked, "How long has she been dead for?"

YOU MUST CHOOSE!

Would you rather...

give oral sex to someone after he/she just had major diarrhea

OR

make out with someone who just threw up?

Would you rather...

receive oral sex from someone who drank too much and then proceeds to throw up on you

OR

be giving oral sex (on your knees) to someone who drank too much and proceeds to throw up on you?

Note: These questions excerpted from Søren Kierkegaard's *Truth and Subjectivity*

YOU MUST CHOOSE!

Would you rather have phone sex with...

Tracy Morgan *OR* Alex Trebek?

Flavor Flav *OR* Lou Dobbs?

the banker from *Deal or No Deal* *OR* the *Muppet Show*'s Swedish Chef?

a telemarketer who is trying to sell you something *OR* someone who then requires you to answer a ten minute survey about your call?

the ghost of Johnny Cash *OR* the ghost of George Washington Carver?

Things to consider: peanut fetish

YOU MUST CHOOSE!

Would you rather have phone sex...

with Alicia Keys *OR* Sarah Silverman?

in Latin *OR* pig-Latin?

with Tyra Banks *OR* JK Rowling?

Would you rather...

have snail mail sex (bawdy letters sent back and forth over a period of months)

OR

have drive-thru intercom sex with a fast food order taker?

YOU MUST CHOOSE!

Would you rather have sex with...

a hot garbage man *OR* an unattractive rock star?

a porn star *OR* a pop star?

a hot dispassionate woman *OR* a down and dirty ugly woman with a unibrow and a goiter on her neck the size of a Dixie cup?

an incredibly witty sumo wrestler *OR* a mysterious and troubled busboy?

a barber shop quartet who make all sexual sounds in harmony *OR* a pack of Ewoks?

YOU MUST CHOOSE!

Would you rather...

have sex with Lady Gaga and then have to wear her outfits for a month

OR

have sex with Dame Judi Dench?

Would you rather...

have sex with the 4 out of 5 dentists that recommend Trident sugarless gum

OR

the 5th dissenting dentist?

Things to consider: Do you like rebels?... Rebels with tooth decay?

YOU MUST CHOOSE!

Getting Technical

Would you rather...

have sex with the fourth image when you google "swarthy"

OR

the third image when you google "albino"?

Make your choice before googling, then check and see what you are dealing with.

Would you rather...

do the Mac guy in a PC way

OR

do the PC guy in a Mac way?

YOU MUST CHOOSE!

Would you rather...

use a vibrator that also acts as an iPod

OR

a vibrator that also works as an alarm clock (insert before you go to sleep and it vibrates at the time you set it for)?

Things to consider: having mood music, cheerful mornings

YOU MUST CHOOSE!

Would you rather...

have sex with Siamese triplet Jessica Albas (male);
Brad Pitts (female)

OR

with just the singular version?

Would you rather...

have sex with a man with a 1-inch penis

OR

a 17-inch penis? Oral sex? Anal sex?

YOU MUST CHOOSE!

Would you rather...

have sex with Rosie O'Donnell

OR

have to push her up a steep hill?

Would you rather...

have sex with Sarah Palin *OR* Tina Fey?

Sarah Palin *OR* Tina Fey if you had to talk for three hours before and after the sex?

Sarah Palin *OR* Tina Fey, if Todd Palin promised to take you out snowmobiling after?

Things to consider: The porn *Who's Nailin' Paylin* was made shortly after her vice-presidential bid. What other political porns can you think of that should be made? Examples: *Ridin' Biden*, *Fuck-with-Me Huckabee*

YOU MUST CHOOSE!

Fun with Puppets

Would you rather...

have sex with Big Bird Oscar the Grouch?

Things to consider: Oscar's bad boy attitude, contracting STDs (Bird Flu, Oscar's lice, etc.)

The Count *OR* Snuffleupagus?

Things to consider: the Count's OCD, Snuffy produces 18 gallons of ejaculate upon orgasm

Would you rather...

masturbate with a real, living Elmo hand puppet

OR

with a living Cookie Monster hand puppet?

Things to consider: Elmo's constant giggling ruining the mood, CM's dangerously voracious appetite

YOU MUST CHOOSE!

Would you rather...

have sex with the offspring of Josh Duhamel and Fergie when it grows up *OR* the offspring of Katie and Tom Cruise?

the offspring of Gisele and Tom Brady *OR* the offspring of Angelina Jolie and Brad Pitt?

the offspring of Danny DeVito and Rhea Perlman *OR* the offspring of past couple Roseanne Barr and Tom Arnold?

Would you rather...

have sex with an auctioneer who speaks in an auctioneer inflection during sex

OR

an aspiring rapper who freestyle rhymes during sex?

YOU MUST CHOOSE!

Where'd You Rather...?

Would you rather have sex...

on the monkey bars *OR* on a seesaw?

on you parents' bed when they are out *OR* in the room adjacent to your parents' room (separated only by a thin wall) while they are home?

in a plane restroom (mile high club) *OR* in a train restroom (4 foot high club)?

in the pit with all those balls in a Chuck E. Cheese play area *OR* in a car wash?

on a bed of nails in private *OR* on a luxuriously soft bed at Mattress Discounters during a Columbus Day sale?

YOU MUST CHOOSE!

Would you rather...

have sex with Bono   *OR*   Elvis in his prime?

Jason Mraz   *OR*   Jack Johnson?

Dave Matthews   *OR*   Rob Thomas?

What if each serenaded you first?

Would you rather...

have sex with Beyoncé   *OR*   Christina Aguilera?

Madonna now   *OR*   Britney when she turns 50?

Amy Winehouse sober   *OR*   Amy Winehouse messed up?

YOU MUST CHOOSE!

Good Sports

Would you rather have sex with...

Danica Patrick *OR* Venus Williams?

an Olympic gymnast *OR* an Olympic figure skater?

Tennis star Maria Sharapova grunting like she does when she plays *OR* hottie golf star Kim Hall as quiet as she is when she golfs?

a beach volleyball player covered in sand *OR* a pro bowler who celebrates upon orgasm like they would when they bowl a strike?

Things to consider: bowler's proclivity for instituting the Shocker, keeping score

YOU MUST CHOOSE!

(im)Perfect Partners

Would you rather...

have a sex partner who always ejaculates prematurely after one minute *OR* one who ejaculates 2 days postmaturely wherever they are?

who only talks dirty in spoonerisms (Example: "Boo me in the dutt." & "Cuck my sock.") *OR* only talks dirty through revolutionary war similes (Example: "Take me, like the British took Bunker Hill on their 3rd attempt in 1775!")

who you are able to apply Photoshop effects to in real life *OR* who could do an impression of anyone perfectly?

Things to consider: Dragon wings would look awesome!; possible impressions: porn stars, movie stars, Don Rickles, your old girlfriend/boyfriend

YOU MUST CHOOSE!

Would you rather...

have sex with Penélope Cruz if she spoke dirty in a Spanish accent *OR* Heidi Klum if she spoke dirty in a frightening German accent ?

Barry Manilow if he then wrote you a love song *OR* Eminem if he then wrote a hateful rap about you?

someone with a perfect body wearing a Hitler mask *OR* someone with a saggy, wrinkly, flabby body wearing an Obama mask?

YOU MUST CHOOSE!

Would you rather...

have sex with Salma Hayek's body but with your face on it

OR

with your body with Salma Hayek's face (genitals remain female)?

Would you rather...

have sex with a half-sized Angelina Jolie

OR

double-sized J.Lo?

YOU MUST CHOOSE!

Would you rather...

French kiss Liza Minnelli *OR* a bowl of sliced jalapeño peppers?

your aunt *OR* a pile of fish hooks?

the inside of a bowling shoe and ball *OR*

_____ ?

(insert the ugliest or most disgusting person you know)

Would you rather...

bang a prize pig at the state fair

OR

the guy running the tilt-a-whirl?

YOU MUST CHOOSE!

Would you rather...

have tender respectful sex with Joe Lieberman

OR

get bukkaked in humiliation by U2?

Building off bukkake, *would you rather...*

get bukkaked by a group of anonymous Japanese businessmen *OR* the cast of *Growing Pains*?

your junior high school teachers *OR* a group of ET's species?

Mötley Crüe *OR* all the Smurfs?

YOU MUST CHOOSE!

Would you rather...

finger Meg Ryan

OR

lick Megan Fox's ass after a ten mile hike?

Would you rather...

be attacked by ninjas while having sex with a supermodel

OR

vice-versa?

YOU MUST CHOOSE!

Would you rather...

have a sex doll in the likeness of Jenna Haze *OR* Wonder Woman?

an anonymous hot woman *OR* the celebrity of your choice?

Harriet Tubman *OR* a Vulcan woman?

Would you rather...

have cowgirl sex with a missionary

OR

missionary sex with a cowgirl?

Things to consider: conversion, spurs

YOU MUST CHOOSE!

CHAPTER TWO

Embarrassing Episodes

Secure in your sexuality? Well, you're about to find out exactly how confident and open you truly are. Cringe and bear these gut-wrenching dilemmas featuring an embarrassment of riches and a richness of embarrassment.

Would you rather...

have all your sexual thoughts automatically tweeted to your parents

OR

vice-versa?

Would you rather...

have your Facebook status always show your latest sexual intercourse duration

OR

have to post at least one picture a month on your Facebook feed from one of your sexual encounters (does not have to show nudity)?

YOU MUST CHOOSE!

Would you rather...

have Ken Burns make a five part documentary on your adolescent masturbation habits to air on PBS

OR

have a complete written transcript of your sexual encounters available for download for $29.99 on npr.com?

Things to consider Doris Kearns Goodwin weighing in on your use of a "slut-sock"; slow dissolves from a still shot of your ecstatic face to a tube of KY Jelly; do people read?

YOU MUST CHOOSE!

Would you rather...

go to the emergency room with a roll of quarters stuck up your ass

OR

your penis stuck in a Heinz Ketchup bottle? (Women substitute second option with "three hard-boiled eggs stuck in your vagina")?

Things to consider: The excuse: "I fell on something." Can you think of other excuses?

Would you rather...

find out your boyfriend/girlfriend had been blogging about your sex life

OR

that your parents have been blogging about theirs?

YOU MUST CHOOSE!

Strip Search

Would you rather...

pole dance naked on a freezing pole

OR

in front of your in-laws?

Things to consider: labia/scrotal adhesion to pole; father-in-law

Would you rather...

strip in front of _____

(insert awkward relative or acquaintance)

OR

have them strip in front of you?

YOU MUST CHOOSE!

Would you rather...

have your Match.com profile written by your mother *OR* father?

your six-year old nephew *OR* your 80-year-old grandmother?

your ex *OR* one of those spam email writers?

Things to consider: bitter comments from your ex; "It is with the utmost sincerity that I request you achieve a date with me. May I introduce myself. I have recently come into some money and need your company and bank routing number..."

YOU MUST CHOOSE!

Would you rather...

have a sex tape turn up on the web of you and an old girlfriend/boyfriend

OR

a sex tape turn up of you and your current girlfriend?

Would you rather...

have your sexual encounters watched and critiqued by a focus group of 18-35-year-old males behind a one-way mirror *OR* watched and graded by your high school gym teacher?

critiqued by a focus group of women 35-49 *OR* men 65-90?

a focus group of girls 12-15 *OR* super-intelligent but loveless robots?

YOU MUST CHOOSE!

Would you rather...

be getting busy with someone for the first time, and as you take their pants off, you see they have the largest amount of pubic hair you have ever seen

a crotch tattoo of Matlock?

Would you rather...

star in a herpes medication commercial as a patient for $50,000

as the doctor for $5,000?

YOU MUST CHOOSE!

Would you rather...

slap your grandmother across the face

OR

watch the Internet video *Two Girls, One Cup* with her?

Would you rather be caught by your partner masturbating to...

pictures of your ex *OR* pictures of your partner's sibling?

a cute 15-year-old *OR* a 90-year-old?

a framed photo of yourself *OR* lascivious pictures of Optimus Prime?

YOU MUST CHOOSE!

Would you rather...

compete in a spelling bee and win, but have a vicious erection the entire time

OR

go out in the first round to spare yourself further embarrassment? (women: substitute super erect nipples)

Would you rather...

the full catalog of your sexual experiences was available for rental on Netflix

OR

the full catalog of your parents' sexual experiences was available?

YOU MUST CHOOSE!

Would you rather...

have your mother have to sign a consent form every time you perform intercourse

OR

have to solve the *New York Times* crossword?

Would you rather...

have your genitalia regularly printed on the backs of milk cartons nationwide

OR

your orgasm become a popular cell phone ring tone?

YOU MUST CHOOSE!

Would you rather...

have one sexual encounter a month reviewed and analyzed by sports commentators on ESPN

OR

have your sex life traded on the New York Stock Exchange and regularly reported on CNBC?

Thing to consider: commentators using the chalkboard, slow-motion replays; Your stockholders furious that you didn't have enough anal in the 4th quarter.

Would you rather...

have your sexual performance criticized by Simon Cowell once a year on national television

OR

by your girlfriend once a week at a family dinner?

YOU MUST CHOOSE!

Would you rather...

knowingly have sex with a trannie once

OR

unknowingly have sex with a trannie for a year?

Would you rather...

walk in on your parents having sex

OR

on your grandparents having sex?

Would you rather...

release a sex tape of you screwing Roseanne Barr

OR

lovingly spooning Dustin Diamond?

YOU MUST CHOOSE!

Which embarrassing fetish would you rather have?

Most robust sexual arousal experienced by defecating in wallets *OR* by dressing up and being treated as a Chinese peasant rice-farmer?

Unwavering need to be called "Leonard" to reach orgasm *OR* be unable to reach orgasm unless you stuff your anal canal with a He-Man doll?

YOU MUST CHOOSE!

Compulsion to dry-hump tortoises *OR* undeniable urge to have intercourse with grocery store gumball machines?

Things to consider: gumball machines are considered to be some of the most germ-infested objects in the world; shell scrapes

Only attracted to freckled, redheaded Asians *OR* albinos under 5'2" with 1400+ SAT scores and O negative blood type?

YOU MUST CHOOSE!

Would you rather...

have your sex life as a topic on *Meet the Press*

OR

TRL?

Would you rather...

get a Dirty Sanchez

OR

not have to undergo any deviant sexual act, but have a new sex act named after you that involves giving an enema of melted cheese to one's partner and then having them rectally squeeze it out on party crackers which you two share while sipping a glass of fine port?

YOU MUST CHOOSE!

Would you rather...

wake up after drunken night to find yourself in bed with your mother's best friend

OR

with a huge back tattoo of Ron Jaworski's face?

Would you rather...

have to watch the Internet vid *Two Girls, One Cup* with your mom

OR

watch *Two Girls, One Cup* starring your mom?

Things to consider: would you kill yourself after the second option?

YOU MUST CHOOSE!

Would you rather...

have a naked pictorial in *Playboy* or *Playgirl*

OR

go on *Dancing with the Stars*? What about *Hustler*? *Swank*? *Juggs*?

Would you rather...

have your sex broadcast on every television at Best Buy in HD

OR

your masturbation fantasies magically converted to video and put on YouTube?

YOU MUST CHOOSE!

CHAPTER 3 THREE

Sex Changes

Your humdrum sex life is about to be made a whole lot more interesting. You are soon to be stricken with a bizarre curse: an irksome inconvenience, a deviant deformity, or an unusual behavioral disorder. In an era where Internet Porn is consumed like a daily vitamin, and a Cleveland Steamer is now considered second base, you might think it would be hard to make your sex life odder than it already is. Guess again.

Would you rather...

the strength of your erection directly correlate to the number of service bars on your cell phone

OR

your erection, like a compass, always points north?

Things to consider: switching to Verizon, camping West Virginia wilderness, "spotty coverage"

Would you rather...

(Women: substitute: "Celebrity gossip" for "porn")

never be able to use the Internet for porn again

OR

never be able to use the Internet for legitimate research again?

YOU MUST CHOOSE!

Would you rather...

orgasm once every five seconds, five minutes, five years

OR

high five?

Things to consider: your job, your marriage, your pick-up basketball games

Would you rather...

have all your sexual experiences narrated like a nature documentary by Sir David Attenborough

OR

sarcastically commented on by the robots from *Mystery Science Theater 3000*?

YOU MUST CHOOSE!

Would you rather...

have nipples that have grown fused into each other like a fleshy handle

OR

have extra nipples in the palms of your hands?

Things to consider: ease of arousal, stumping palm-readers, shaking hands at business meetings

Would you rather...

live with a permanent erection of one inch

OR

19 inches?

Things to consider: sex, potential for injury, tucking into your sock

YOU MUST CHOOSE!

Would you rather...

have a maximum time limit of 3 minutes to complete all your sex acts

OR

a minimum time of 3 hours (if you climax before then you have to start over)?

Would you rather have to seduce women using only...

origami **OR** shadow puppets?

a kazoo **OR** your testicles?

Saved by the Bell trivia **OR** prop comedy?

YOU MUST CHOOSE!

Would you rather your porn name be...

First name = your middle name; Last name = the first street you grew up on

OR

First name = favorite meteorological adjective (Stormy, Misty, Snowy, Dewy); Last name = favorite substance (Diamond, Stone, Wood, etc.)?

First name = state you're from; Last name = surname of the celebrity you most look like

OR

First name = any NyQuil-alleviated symptom (Stuffy, Coughing, Sneezing, Aching, etc); last name = Last name of closest Jewish friend?

YOU MUST CHOOSE!

Would you rather...

your orgasm face appear on all your photo IDs

OR

always exhibit a perfect emotionless poker face and speak in a monotone during all romance and sex?

Would you rather...

make a progressively higher-pitched, whistling teakettle sound as you approach orgasm

OR

feel the kickback force of a shotgun when climaxing?

YOU MUST CHOOSE!

Right before you approach orgasm, would you rather...

have your adorable pet kitten nuzzle up against you

OR

have your grandmother leave an audible message on your answering machine?

Would you rather...

cry semen and ejaculate tears

OR

sneeze semen and ejaculate mucus?

Things to consider: trying to have a child, tearjerker movies, risk of ocular gonorrhea, crusting facials

YOU MUST CHOOSE!

Would you rather...

during sex, thrust to the rhythm of the opening bars of "Eye of the Tiger"

OR

compulsively apologize after each thrust?

Would you rather...

have the only foreplay that works for you be eyeball stimulation

OR

having your partner fake you out by pretending to throw a tennis ball?

Things to consider: optometrist visits, challenge/pleasure of taking your contacts out, "Where'd it go? Where'd that ball go?! Yay!"

YOU MUST CHOOSE!

Would you rather...

have a bizarre condition where your penis is 12 inches when limp but only 3 inches when erect

OR

one that is 28 inches limp and 6 inches erect?

Things to consider: tying it around your waist like a sweatshirt; rolling it up like a snail shell

Would you rather...

ejaculate with one fine line of fluid like a squirt gun

OR

in a wide "shotgun blast" of fluid?

YOU MUST CHOOSE!

Would you rather...

only be able to have one sexual partner your whole life

OR

be able to have sex with any person only once but have no restrictions on number of partners?

Would you rather...

(men) be celibate except one day per decade with your choice of Victoria Secret supermodel *OR* be married to a nymphomaniac Kirstie Alley?

(women) your choice of movie star once per decade *OR* be married to a sexually charged Al Roker?

YOU MUST CHOOSE!

Would you rather...

have your genitals located on the small of your back

OR

on your left shoulder?

Would you rather...

permanently have your genitals shifted 3 inches to the left
OR rotated 40 degrees counter-clockwise?

4 inches to the left *OR* 180 degrees rotated?

3 inches to the left *OR* 3 inches higher up?

YOU MUST CHOOSE!

Which of the following strange venereal diseases would you endure if you had to choose one?

- Alaskan King Crabs

- Eyeball herpes

- Constantly Expanding Testicles

- an STD that makes the sound of a bagpipe when you defecate

- an STD that makes your genitals ooze pickle juice

- an STD that makes your penis lighter than air

- an STD that makes your penis a tension-coiled spring like an April Fool's peanut brittle novelty snake

- an STD that makes you think you are Federal Reserve Chairman Ben Bernanke during sex

YOU MUST CHOOSE!

Would you rather...

'70s porn music magically play any time you have sex

OR

have it play every time you say something that could be interpreted as double entendre no matter where you are?

Things to consider: I just need to "file this memo."

Would you rather...

be compelled to dry-hump anyone you encounter wearing a visor

OR

be completely unrecognizable unless your genitals are exposed?

YOU MUST CHOOSE!

Would you rather...

have all attractive people be severely allergic to your genitals

OR

all of your sexual partners henceforth develop Post Traumatic Stress Disorder?

Would you rather...

have your climax always interrupted by a phone call from your mom

OR

by Kanye West rushing in and saying, "I'ma let you finish..." and then launching into some inappropriate speech?

YOU MUST CHOOSE!

Would you rather...

never be able to watch porn again for the rest of your life

OR

only be able to watch porn for the rest of your life?

Would you rather...

sex always take as long as completing the *TV Guide* crossword puzzle

OR

the *New York Times* crossword puzzle?

YOU MUST CHOOSE!

Would you rather...

only be able to utter state capitals while climaxing *OR* only be able to utter Biblical quotes?

Greek Gods *OR* your own name?

"Here comes the trolley!" *OR* the song "Flash Gordon" by Queen?

Would you rather...

have breast implants filled with M&M's *OR* peanut M&M's?

Uranium *OR* termites?

an entire world like that on the flower in *Horton Hears a Who* *OR* the spirit of Leif Ericson?

YOU MUST CHOOSE!

Would you rather...

fart maple syrup *OR* nitrous oxide?

flames *OR* thumbtacks?

Seinfeld one-liners *OR* flu vaccines?

Would you rather...

have genitalia made of fine crystal which if shattered cannot be repaired

OR

warped imperfect genitalia made from a clay mold that a 6-year-old attempted to accurately craft?

YOU MUST CHOOSE!

Nipples!

Would you rather...

have nipples that grow an inch a day for the rest of your life and curl up all crazy like those dudes who never cut their fingernails *OR* have perpetually lactating nipples (PLN's)?

Things to consider: babies suckling through crazy straw-like nipples, work as a barrista

have literal silver dollar nipples *OR* literal pencil eraser nipples?

nipples that can be shot as poisonous darts *OR* as grappling hooks?

YOU MUST CHOOSE!

Would you rather...

during sexual congress, be unable to get Burl Ives' "Holly Jolly Christmas" out of your head

OR

be unable to shake the image of the Harlem Globetrotters?

Would you rather...

while in the throes of passion, accidentally yell out the name of your ex

OR

your partner's mother?

YOU MUST CHOOSE!

Would you rather...

temporarily switch faces with your partner every time you have sex

OR

temporarily add 50 years to both your ages?

Would you rather...

upon orgasm, ejaculate a cup of honey

OR

a gallon of gasoline?

Things to consider: tea, rising gas prices, bear attacks, your carbon footprint.

YOU MUST CHOOSE!

Urethra Franklin

 Would you rather...
your urethra quadruple in size

OR

shrink to the size of a pin hole?

 Would you rather...
have four penis holes on the top of your shaft like a flute

OR

dozens of holes in the tip like a shower head?

YOU MUST CHOOSE!

Would you rather...

(Men) have a 3" bigger penis *OR* have a lover with DD breasts?

(Women): have a lover with a 3" bigger penis *OR* you have natural DD breasts?

Would you rather...

have to use porn from the 1950's *OR* porn sent back from the 2150's?

European porn with weird overly vocal dudes *OR* porn without sound?

porn with flagrant product placement *OR* porn where every scene is preceded and followed by a clip of Al Gore reminding you about climate change?

a magazine called "Celebrity Skin Grafts" *OR* "Asymmetrical Juggs"?

YOU MUST CHOOSE!

Would you rather...

orgasm at every mention of the economy

OR

only become sexually aroused within a quarter mile of an Arby's?

Would you rather...

always have to be on your back during sex

OR

always have to face Mecca?

YOU MUST CHOOSE!

Would you rather...

have sex with a girl who has blinding search lights for breasts

OR

a wise-cracking vagina?

Would you rather...

be unable to tell the difference between your keys and a dildo

OR

your wallet and a pocket pussy?

Things to consider: business meetings, getting the check at a restaurant, getting locked out

YOU MUST CHOOSE!

Dirty Talk

Would you rather...

have a partner who talks dirty in a low mumble that is hard to hear *OR* in the unnecessarily extra loud inflection people use when on cell phones outdoors?

who talks dirty in sign language *OR* who takes a while to answer your dirty comments and questions like they are on a satellite delay?

who talks dirty by writing on cue cards *OR* in binary?

who talks dirty in Chinese *OR* beatnik poetry?

YOU MUST CHOOSE!

If you had to choose one of the following to use as birth control, which would you choose?

- A Jellyfish
- A catcher's mitt
- Scotch tape and a banana peel
- Contraceptive SpongeBob

YOU MUST CHOOSE!

Would you rather...

have an incredible-looking body that is completely sexually nonfunctional

OR

a hideous-looking body that performs amazingly sexually and experiences terrific sensation?

Would you rather...

have cowbells for nipple piercings

OR

pieces of string with helium balloons on the end?

YOU MUST CHOOSE!

Pick-a-Penis!

Would you rather...

Women: Read as "have a partner with..."

a penis that is coated with chloroform *OR* one that requires the use of a bike tire pump to get erect?

a penis that looks like a Native American totem pole *OR* like the old puzzle: The Missing Link?

a light-saber penis *OR* a branding iron penis with your initials on the head?

a penis with a tiny rhinoceros horn on the tip *OR* a penis that wriggles like a snake whenever you hear music?

YOU MUST CHOOSE!

Vexing Vaginas!

Would you rather...

Men: Read as "have a partner with..."

have a greeting card microchip implanted in your vagina that plays "Feliz Navidad" every time you spread your legs

OR one that blows with the force of a leaf-blower every other minute?

Things to consider: being "blown out", using a hose to blow your hair, positions that keep the legs closed

Would you rather...

have a vagina that shoots a barrage of camera flashes like the paparazzi when it gets aroused *OR*

one that attracts the paparazzi when it gets aroused?

Things to consider: obstacles to oral sex, pictures on gossip sites

YOU MUST CHOOSE!

If you had to choose one of the following pubic haircuts, which would you choose?

- The Don King
- Flock of Seagulls
- Corn Rows
- Lionel Richie-style Jheri curls
- 1880's Circus Muscleman Handlebar Mustache

YOU MUST CHOOSE!

Would you rather...

(men) have your testicles and eyeballs exchange places

OR

your nose and penis?

Things to consider: scrotal surgery to create transparent holes, erections, perineum odor

Would you rather...

(women) have your nipples and eyes change places

OR

your vagina and nose?

Things to consider: cutting holes in shirts, moving to the Middle East to wear burqas and veils

Note: These questions excerpted from Jean-Paul Sartre's *Being and Nothingness*

YOU MUST CHOOSE!

Would you rather...

be a coprophiliac

OR

an urolagniac?

Guess first and then look them up.

Would you rather...

with every orgasm, have your skin pigmentation of your genitals, nipples and anus turn a shade lighter

OR

a shade darker?

YOU MUST CHOOSE!

Ejacu-tastic!

Would you rather...

ejaculate skunk spray *OR* Krazy Glue?

pepper spray *OR* a freeze ray?

Things to consider: crime-fighting

sperm in geltabs which dissolve in twenty minutes
OR the sound of an air horn?

YOU MUST CHOOSE!

Would you rather...

have pubic hair all over your head (including facial hair if you are a guy)

OR

all over your body?

Would you rather...

spend the next 15 years going through puberty again

OR

go through reverse puberty at age 40?

YOU MUST CHOOSE!

Would you rather...

always have to have sex in a public place

OR

in a refrigerator (shelves removable)?

Would you rather...

be able to only have sex in laundry rooms

OR

have to have sex everyday at 8 a.m. or you will die?

Things to consider: extra rinse cycle; Daylight Savings Time.

YOU MUST CHOOSE!

Would you rather...

have a vagina in each armpit

OR

one little vagina in your belly button?

Would you rather...

whenever you get sexually aroused, the only way to relieve yourself is to dry hump a poster of Mr. Spock

OR

only be able to reach orgasm by making it through the third screen on Donkey Kong?

YOU MUST CHOOSE!

Would you rather...

for 3 full days after every orgasm, become completely illiterate

OR

have your credit score negatively impacted every time you receive oral sex?

Things to consider: How would this impact the frequency of each?

Would you rather...

only be able to have sex in the same room as a sleeping relative

OR

inside city dumpsters?

YOU MUST CHOOSE!

Would you rather...

have an extra nose on your forehead

OR

on your taint?

 Would you rather...

have a penis sticking out of the top of your head

OR

have assholes all over your back?

Things to consider: pompadours, comb-overs, taking dumps would resemble Whack-a-Mole

YOU MUST CHOOSE!

Would you rather...

defecate dreidels

OR

fresh scallops?

Would you rather...

have your fingers always smell like bacon

OR

vagina?

YOU MUST CHOOSE!

Would you rather...

have three testicles *OR* one?

have three nipples *OR* one?

four testicles in two scrotums *OR* all in one scrotum?

YOU MUST CHOOSE!

Would you rather...

have a two-pronged penis

OR

a penis with many smaller penises inside it like Russian nesting dolls?

Things to consider: removing shells to fit the woman/orifice

Would you rather...

have a week taken off the end of your life every time you have sex

OR

a day off your life every time you masturbate?

Things to consider: It's simple math.

YOU MUST CHOOSE!

Would you rather...

document the circumstances of your last 20 orgasms on your resumé

OR

leave five exes as references for sexual performance?

Would you rather...

only be able to have sex with ex-cons

OR

ex-pats

OR

X-Men?

YOU MUST CHOOSE!

Would you rather...

be uncontrollably sexually attracted to cashiers

OR

funeral pallbearers?

Which movie line would you exclaim upon orgasm:

"Are you not entertained!"

"King Kong ain't got shit on me!"

"With great power comes great responsibility"

"I drink your milkshake"

"I'm the king of the world!"

YOU MUST CHOOSE!

Would you rather...

have a partner who is cold and listless as a ship dead in the water

OR

one that always wants to use whips, chains, candles and instruments of pain and degradation on you?

Would you rather...

orgasm every time you sneeze

OR

sneeze every time you orgasm?

YOU MUST CHOOSE!

CHAPTER FOUR

Fantasies & Powers

Admit it. You fantasize about sex. We all do. It's nothing to be ashamed of. It's just fantasy. Until now, that is. The following dilemmas offer the chance to realize one of two fantasies or sexual super powers; sometimes wild, sometime mild, always interesting.

Would you rather...

play 18 holes with Tiger Woods

OR

play 18 mistress holes with Tiger Woods?

Things to consider: playing in the rough, ball-washers, other obvious golf jokes

Would you rather...

be visited by the "Ghost of Your Sexual Experiences Past"

OR

the "Ghost of Your Sexual Experiences Future"?

Things to consider: What would each show you? What would you learn from it?

YOU MUST CHOOSE!

Would you rather...

(Men: Read as "have a partner with...")
have a vagina that can magically validate any parking pass

OR

that can comfortably hold all the contents of your purse?

Would you rather...

have a penis that comes in handy as a bottle opener

OR

a cigarette lighter?

YOU MUST CHOOSE!

Would you rather...

be able to make sexual organs taste like anything you want

OR

have the golden touch where every breast you touch permanently becomes a perfect size DD?

Things to consider: touching your own breasts, touching your partner's; dark chocolate, peppermint, turkey with gravy

Would you rather...

every penis you touch becomes permanently 14 inches long

OR

every penis you touch becomes 2 inches long?

Things to consider: exacting revenge, your partner, yourself, running a business

YOU MUST CHOOSE!

Animation Animals!

Would you rather...

titty-fuck Jessica Rabbit

OR

fin-fuck the Little Mermaid?

Would you rather...

get ravaged by the beast in *Beauty and the Beast*

OR

get nose-fucked by a lying Pinocchio?

Things to consider: using the B&B's animated inanimate objects to enhance the pleasure; perverted Geppetto watching?

Would you rather...

go to a strip club where all the strippers are crushes you had in high school

OR

a strip club where all the strippers say what they are actually thinking?

Would you rather...

have everyone you've ever pleasured yourself to appear at Thanksgiving dinner

OR

be able to download a catalog of erotic dream scenarios into your brain?

Things consider: "enjoy the stuffing", "leg or breast?", Ben Wa brussels sprouts

YOU MUST CHOOSE!

Would you rather...

have sex with Sigourney Weaver from the original *Aliens*

OR

Sigourney Weaver as the 10-foot-tall blue alien in *Avatar*?

Would you rather...

have sex with Zachary Quinto's Spock

OR

Leonard Nimoy's?

YOU MUST CHOOSE!

Fantasies & Powers

Fantasies & Powers

Back that App Up!

Would you rather...

have an "app" that tells you the ovulation and STD status of one-night stands

OR

the number of times she's been dumped for "being crazy?"

Would you rather...

have and app that tells you the size of a man's junk

OR

that translates what a guy is saying to what he is actually thinking?

YOU MUST CHOOSE!

Your attractive friends invite you and your partner to have group sex.

Would you rather...

participate

OR

not?

Would you rather...

have an extra set of your gender's genitals anywhere you choose on your body

OR

have the addition of the opposite gender's genitals somewhere on your body?

Things to consider: three-ways, one-ways, rainy days

YOU MUST CHOOSE!

Would you rather...

watch Britney Spears and Christina Aguilera in a UFC match-up

OR

the Fridge and Manute Bol?

Would you rather...

have a really smart bomb-sniffing dog who can locate anyone who would be attracted to you

OR

have a magical inch worm who can locate any g-spot?

YOU MUST CHOOSE!

Would you rather...

have every part of your body be as pleasure-sensitive as your genitals

OR

not?

Would you rather...

be able to make the people from any Internet porn clip appear in your room

OR

while watching any TV show, be able to make the characters launch into some hardcore action?

Things to consider: *McLaughlin Group Orgies*

YOU MUST CHOOSE!

Which porno would you most want to watch, imagining what the plot would be?

- *The Fast and Bicurious*
- *Womb Raider*
- *Schindler's Fist*
- *The Incredible Bulge*—(penis turns green and rips through clothes when excited)
- *The Little Sperm Maid*—(animation)
- *Semento*—(told backwards from ejaculation all the way to putting clothes back on)
- *The Firm*

YOU MUST CHOOSE!

Would you rather...

be able to perform oral sex on yourself

OR

be able to perform oral sex once on your celebrity crush?

Would you rather use as a sex toy...

Snuggie or menorah?

Weebles or hand saw?

cafeteria tray or credenza?

YOU MUST CHOOSE!

World's Best Venereal Diseases

Which of the following would you most want to have?

- Genital diamonds
- Sexually Transmitted MP3's
- The Clap-on Clap-off Clap
- Vaginal ATM
- Free Carpool Lane Gonorrhea

YOU MUST CHOOSE!

Would you rather...

have IM sex

have UPS chart sex where you draw doodles that become dirty by erasing or adding lines?

Which would you rather use as an erotic food to enhance sex?

Whipped Cream *OR* melted chocolate?

A-1 sauce *OR* hard-boiled eggs?

Fun Dip *OR* gobstoppers?

YOU MUST CHOOSE!

Would you rather star in a porn directed by...

Quentin Tarantino *OR* Woody Allen?

Peter Jackson *OR* Larry David?

Todd Phillips *OR* John Woo?

Yourself *OR* Pixar?

YOU MUST CHOOSE!

Would you rather...

plant an herb garden with Mandy Moore

OR

ride a freight train with Katherine Heigl?

Would you rather...

make a frittata with Philip Seymour Hoffman

OR

play Mastermind with Clint Eastwood?

YOU MUST CHOOSE!

Would you rather...

have sex with Taylor Swift, swiftly

OR

Jenna Haze, hazily?

Would you rather...

once a day, feel the sensation of a good orgasm

OR

the feeling you got when you were a kid and you awoke to find it snowing outside and that school was cancelled?

YOU MUST CHOOSE!

Would you rather watch a discovered sex tape with...

Brad Pitt and Angelina Jolie *OR* Barack and Michelle Obama?

Yao Ming and Christina Ricci *OR* Tracy Morgan and Vanessa Hudgens?

the contestants on the last *Biggest Loser* (pre-weight loss) in an orgy *OR* your parents?

Johnny Depp and Julia Child *OR* the Gumbel brothers and Eliza Dushku?

YOU MUST CHOOSE!

Would you rather...

"three hole punch" Sarah Palin

OR

give a pearl necklace to her oldest daughter?

Would you rather...

be able to change anyone's name legally to the porn star name of your choice

OR

be given $20,000?

Things to consider: White House Press Secretary Robert Gibbs is now Dick Jammer; Steve Harwood is now Steve Hardwood.

YOU MUST CHOOSE!

Would you rather...

screw a janitor on a space ship

OR

an astronaut in a janitor's closet?

Would you rather...

have a lover that performs oral on you whenever you want

OR

one that makes you a burrito and then lets you go to sleep after sex?

YOU MUST CHOOSE!

Would you rather...

have a nationally touring ballet based on your life

OR

get a footjob from one of the ballerinas?

Would you rather...

be able to give anyone an instant hard-on

OR

have an anus that manicures nails?

YOU MUST CHOOSE!

Who would you rather have in your bedroom during sex:

a wise grizzled golf caddy who stands by the side of the bed and offers you tips on your form *OR* a tennis ball boy who quickly sprints across the bed and puts it back in anytime it slips out?

the ghost of Ed McMahon to cheer for and corroborate you ("Yesss!") *OR* a JetBlue flight attendant to thank your guest for choosing you and offer him or her a complimentary beverage?

YOU MUST CHOOSE!

Which would you rather have happen to Osama Bin Laden?

have a glass beaker shoved up his pecker and then shattered *OR* 1 million termites climb into his rectum and devour him from the inside out?

have him develop the world's worst case of testicular elephantiasis *OR* become the "bitch" of a San Quentin prison inmate named Jamal?

have him sodomized by a pack mule *OR* have him discover he has been eating pulled pork sandwiches for a year without realizing it?

YOU MUST CHOOSE!

Would you rather...

have vibrating fingers

OR

a vibrating tongue?

Things to consider: Does your answer change if you can't turn them off?

Would you rather...

have group sex with the Pussycat Dolls

OR

the Spice Girls?

YOU MUST CHOOSE!

Would you rather...

have sex with Jennifer Aniston with H1N1

OR

let Jennifer Garner give you butterfly kisses with pinkeye?

Would you rather...

be able to perform close-up magic with your genitals

OR

throw your voice so it appears to be coming out of people's asses?

YOU MUST CHOOSE!

Would you rather...

have any member of the opposite sex's thoughts text messaged to you at any time

OR

be able to control any member of the opposite sex for up to an hour using a Sony Playstation video game controller?

Would you rather...

have a sexual partner who will never have intercourse with you but will give you oral sex whenever you wanted

OR

have a partner who you had the best sex ever imaginable with, but could only have it once a week (and no oral)?

YOU MUST CHOOSE!

Would you rather...

have Wolverine-type retractable claws made of penises

OR

not?

Would you rather...

go to a bachelor party thrown by Genghis Kahn

OR

by Jabba the Hutt?

Things to consider: the Mongol Horde is a potential sausage fest, keg stands with Boba Fett

YOU MUST CHOOSE!

Who would make the best lesbian porn?

Number Six and Boomer from *Battlestar Galactica*?

Ginger and Mary Ann from *Gilligan's Island*?

Pocahontas and the chick from Disney's *Aladdin*?

YOU MUST CHOOSE!

Who would make the best gay porn?

Karl Malone and John Stockton?

Ronald Reagan and Mikhail Gorbachev?

Statler and Waldorf (the *Muppet Show* critics up in the balcony)?

YOU MUST CHOOSE!

Would you rather...

have sex with Jennifer Hudson

OR

pop Megan Fox's back zits?

Would you rather...

get a dick-in-a-box from Justin Timberlake

OR

Nick Lachey's balls in a decorative gift bag?

YOU MUST CHOOSE!

Would you rather...

have a penis where every time it gets rubbed, it summons a genie

OR

that ejaculates three gallons of premium gasoline?

Would you rather...

have breasts with built-in thermostats that keep you warm in the winter and cool in the summer

OR

a hover vagina?

Things to consider: lower heating bill, faster commute

YOU MUST CHOOSE!

Scrotum!

Would you rather...

have a zip-up change purse scrotum

OR

have a scrotum that blows up and expands into a beanbag chair?

Would you rather...

have an elastic scrotum that can be used as a nunchucks-like weapon to fight crime

OR

one made of that stress ball material that you can squeeze to reduce stress?

Note: This page reprinted with permission from William Shakespeare's *The Tempest*.

YOU MUST CHOOSE!

Would you rather...

that all women in the world were required to return phone calls, no matter what

OR

that all women in the world had vaginas that recorded high scores like video games, so you enter your initials afterward and try to break your records?

Would you rather...

have access to a Facebook for sex, where you can log in and see everyone your friends have had sex with, your friends' friends, the whole world interlocking in six degrees of separation

OR

one hour per day of unlimited *Star Trek* Holodeck privileges?

YOU MUST CHOOSE!

5

Down and Dirty: Painful, Gross and Generally Unpleasant ☺

Would you rather... write questions that pander to the lowest common denominator against your own artistic inclinations or write questions that appeal to the worst and most base aspects of humanity: the gross, the lurid, the painful, and the violent? Things to consider: The two are not mutually exclusive. Enjoy.

Would you rather...

take it in the crapper

OR

on the crapper?

Would you rather use as eyedrops...

semen

OR

Tabasco sauce?

YOU MUST CHOOSE!

Would you rather start going down on a girl...

only to see a saturated maxi pad *OR* hermaphroditic genitalia?

only to notice large STD pustules oozing pus *OR* only to find a cockroach slowly emerge from her vagina?

only to see the top of a baby's head starting to crown *OR* only to look up and see your aunt's face?

YOU MUST CHOOSE!

Would you rather...

shit out 100 jacks

OR

a whole winter squash?

Would you rather...

drink a pint of lukewarm asparagus pee

OR

16 ounces of chilled ball sweat?

YOU MUST CHOOSE!

"Best" of "Bestiality"

Would you rather...

blow a chipmunk for twenty minutes

OR

an elephant for one minute?

Would you rather...

manually stimulate a camel to completion

OR

fist an aardwolf?

YOU MUST CHOOSE!

Would you rather...

groom a volatile gorilla

OR

the dingleberries from Michael Moore's ass hair?

Would you rather...

have an adult circumcision

OR

cut off your left pinky?

YOU MUST CHOOSE!

In a pinch, would you rather...

have to get off by using an old lady's used dentures

OR

by slathering your genitalia in fish food and swimming in a salmon hatchery?

In a pinch, would you rather...

get off by covering your parts in peanut butter and birdseed and laying in naked in your backyard

OR

by using one of those public bathroom air-dryers?

YOU MUST CHOOSE!

Would you rather...

fall off a ladder and catch your eyelid on a nail

OR

catch your scrotum on it?

Would you rather...

play "Soggy Biscuit" and lose

OR

get off first?

Things to consider: What would each say about you?

YOU MUST CHOOSE!

Would you rather...

suck on John Travolta's man tits

OR

be Arabian-goggled by Artie Lange?

Would you rather...

have reciprocal "dog in a bathtub" sessions with your next door neighbor

OR

receive a Cleveland Steamer from your neighbors across the street?

YOU MUST CHOOSE!

Would you rather...

pierce your perineum

OR

your uvula?

Would you rather...

have your urethra hole spackled shut

OR

your ass spackled shut?

YOU MUST CHOOSE!

Would you rather...

spend a day having to clean up peep show booths with nothing but your bare hands

OR

spend it cleaning the stadium toilet stall seats the same way after a New England Patriots football game?

Would you rather...

run and slide head first across a Slip N' Slide covered with buffalo semen

OR

fall into a dunk tank of menstrual blood?

YOU MUST CHOOSE!

Would you rather...

set off a mouse trap with your penis

OR

a bear trap with your leg?

Would you rather...

block a punt with your nuts

OR

face?

YOU MUST CHOOSE!

Would you rather...

eat a candied apple covered with a dried semen shell

OR

a bowl of ice cream rolled in pubes?

Would you rather...

when constipated, have your anus snaked out by a plumber

OR

flushed out with a bottle of Drano?

YOU MUST CHOOSE!

Relatively Speaking

Would you rather...

stick your tongue in a hornet's nest *OR*
your grandma's mouth?

make out with a lip-sore-laden homeless man *OR*
your brother?

see your girlfriend in a sex video on the web *OR*
your mom in a *Girls Gone Wild* tape?

be caught masturbating by your mom *OR*
catch your mom masturbating? Dad? Aunt? Grandfather?
Dog? Ben Kingsley?

YOU MUST CHOOSE!

Would you rather...

be the biggest person at a midget orgy

OR

the youngest person at a nursing home orgy?

Would you rather...

dip your balls in boiling oil for five seconds

OR

have a circus strongman grab your ass cheeks and attempt to rip them in half like a phonebook for 30 seconds?

Note: In the Bible, God asks Abraham to bear both in order to prove his faith.

YOU MUST CHOOSE!

Would you rather...

wear a dead fish as a necklace for 10 days

OR

stick a live fish up your ass for 10 seconds?

Would you rather...

play a round of Russian roulette

OR

spend a night in the jail from *Oz*?

YOU MUST CHOOSE!

Would you rather...

read in your grandma's diary explicit details of how she used to derive enormous pleasure from dropping a load in your grandpa's mouth

OR

how she once helped kill a man?

Would you rather...

during sex, have your dog lick your genitals once quickly

OR

lift its leg and urinate on you?

YOU MUST CHOOSE!

Loving Lepers

Would you rather...

make out with a leper and have their tongue come off in your mouth

OR

be feeling up a leper and have their nipple slide off in your hand?

Things to consider: For those who are old enough to remember: Why did the book *Truly Tasteless Jokes* have an entire leper section? It made you think lepers were still a significant demographic in the world. Are they? Have we just forgotten about this forgotten plight?

YOU MUST CHOOSE!

While you're having sex, would you rather watch...

massive head wound surgery *OR* an entire debate between Michael Dukakis and George H. W. Bush?

baby seals being killed for their fur *OR* a 300-pound woman shower?

Two Girls, One Cup *OR* 9/11 footage?

YOU MUST CHOOSE!

Pubes!

Would you rather...

have your grandma knit you a scarf from her pubic hair
that you have to wear every time you see her

OR

get hair plugs from your own pubic hair?

Would you rather...

have your pubes braided by your mom

OR

vice versa?

YOU MUST CHOOSE!

Would you rather...

have the head of your penis slammed with a hammer

OR

stick 25 thumbtacks in your sack and use it
for a pin cushion?

Would you rather...

see how many grapes you can fit into your mouth

OR

in your rectum?

Things to consider: choking, making wine

YOU MUST CHOOSE!

Would you rather...

get dumped on the Jumbotron at a baseball game

OR

by seeing your girlfriend's/boyfriend's Facebook status changed to "single?"

Would you rather...

watch *The Notebook* 20 times in a row

OR

eat 20 pounds of butter?

YOU MUST CHOOSE!

Would you rather...

lick Mo'Nique's asscrack

OR

a mound of bat guano?

Would you rather...

have your family jewels crushed by a steam roller

OR

pecked by birds until nothing was left?

YOU MUST CHOOSE!

Would you rather...

put your penis on a hot grill for 20 seconds

OR

shave off your nipples with a razor blade?

Would you rather...

drink a small glass of your own blood

OR

a tablespoon of your own cum?

YOU MUST CHOOSE!

Would You Rather...? Dirty Version

Would you rather...

pass a marble through your penis

OR

a wiffle ball through your ass?

Would you rather...

pose naked for an art class

OR

go to the beach in a thong for a whole day?

YOU MUST CHOOSE!

Would you rather...

eat raw horse

OR

cooked human flesh?

Would you rather...

stick your dick in a fan

OR

your finger in Tom Bergeron?

YOU MUST CHOOSE!

Animal Instincts

 Would you rather...

have a lobster snap its claw onto your right nipple

OR

a jellyfish drag across your crotch?

Would you rather...

make out with a camel's mouth

OR

a cat's ass?

YOU MUST CHOOSE!

Would you rather...

butt-dial your girlfriend/boyfriend while you're complaining about them

OR

accidentally "sext" your mom?

Would you rather...

be fisted by Edward Scissorhands

OR

given oral by Johnny Staplermouth?

YOU MUST CHOOSE!

Would you rather...

lick Courtney Love's vibrator

OR

Tom Selleck's moustache?

Would you rather...

wring the sweat from an offensive lineman's jock strap into your mouth

OR

shave, dipping and rinsing your razor in an old man's used bedpan?

YOU MUST CHOOSE!

Would you rather...

be tea-bagged by Chuck Norris

OR

take a Norris punch to the jaw?

Would you rather...

sleep on a bed of castrated bull testicles

OR

bathe in a warm bath of mucus?

YOU MUST CHOOSE!

Would you rather...

be caught masturbating to pictures of your ex

OR

the Hamburglar?

Would you rather...

get dog-in-a-bath-tub'd by Brian Williams

OR

jelly-doughnuted by Wilford Brimley?

YOU MUST CHOOSE!

Would you rather...

have your testicles removed and your scrotal sac filled with almonds *OR* magnets?

hydrogen *OR* steel?

glow-worms *OR* Silly Putty?

Would you rather...

floss with a pubic hair every day

OR

wipe your ass with sandpaper?

YOU MUST CHOOSE!

Would you rather...

eat chili-cheese fries smothered in dark pubes

OR

a urine-soaked Twinkie?

Would you rather...

drink a glass of paint

OR

drink a cum fart?

This page excerpted with permission from Aristotle's *Nicomachean Ethics*.

YOU MUST CHOOSE!

Would you rather...

receive an enema from Carrot Top with accompanying prop comedy

OR

get a prostate exam/papsmear administered by Tom Brokaw, followed by a nifty pedal-boat ride?

Would you rather...

give a hot oil massage to Danny Bonaduce

OR

pay a $15,000 fine?

YOU MUST CHOOSE!

Would you rather...

pierce a metal rod through the tip of your penis

OR

through your nose (you can't remove it)?

Would you rather...

for the rest of your life, sleep like Luke Skywalker inside the belly of a Tauntaun

OR

with your parents in the same bed?

YOU MUST CHOOSE!

Would you rather...

get fisted by an orangutan

OR

trunked by an elephant?

Would you rather...

stick your penis in a garbage disposal for 30 seconds

OR

in your _____ 's mouth?
(insert someone gross)

Things to consider: Too much?

YOU MUST CHOOSE!

Would you rather...

mistakenly replace your sex lube with Superglue

OR

your toilet paper with duct tape?

Would you rather...

use a poison ivy condom

OR

have a sushi chef pack your pee-hole with fresh wasabi?

YOU MUST CHOOSE!

Would you rather...

have your exes collaborate on a hate blog about you

OR

be blasted by a Super Soaker full of sloth semen?

Would you rather...

have to walk around with a speculum in your rectum for a day

OR

a golf ball in your mouth?

Things to consider: *There's a Speculum in your Rectum* is a lost Dr. Seuss book.

YOU MUST CHOOSE!

Would you rather eat...

an éclair full of semen *OR* a hot dog topped with fecal "chili"?

snot crème brulee *OR* turd tamale?

vomited venison *OR* lactated-on-lima beans?

pizza topped with fish eyes *OR* spaghetti topped with shaved dead foot skin in place of parmesan cheese?

YOU MUST CHOOSE!

Would you rather wipe your ass with...

poison ivy *OR* dry ice?

a split habanero pepper *OR* your bare hand?

a steel wool pad *OR* your cat?

Would you rather...

die by a bullet to the head

OR

by slow asphyxiation by a large '70s vagina?

YOU MUST CHOOSE!

Would you rather...

get Hot Karled by the creatures in *Where the Wild Things Are*

OR

get leg-humped by ten *Twilight* werewolves?

Would you rather...

get your finger run over by an ice skater

OR

get your balls run over by a roller-blader?

YOU MUST CHOOSE!

If you really wanted a job, would you rather...

conduct a job interview, hanging brain

OR

bleeding profusely from the head?

Would you rather...

eat broccoli out of a girl's vagina

OR

eat chocolate out of a girl's ass?

YOU MUST CHOOSE!

Fun with Grandmas

Would you rather...

blind-side tackle your grandma

OR

give her ten seconds of mouth to mouth with just a tad of tongue?

Would you rather...

watch your grandma strip

OR

be blindfolded and get a lap dance from her?

YOU MUST CHOOSE!

Would you rather suck on...

your high school English teacher's nipples *OR* frog intestines?

a hair clump from a college dorm shower drain *OR* a red hot branding iron?

a woodblock *OR* the bust of Alfred, Lord Tennyson?

YOU MUST CHOOSE!

Would you rather...

find out that your partner starred in a movie called *Rectum Wreckers*

OR

that your mom did? Your dad?

Would you rather anally insert...

a bundle of asparagus *OR* 3 Koosh balls?

a harmonica *OR* a pocket flashlight, handle first?

a Sharpie with the cap off *OR* a hot pepper?

YOU MUST CHOOSE!

Would you rather...

have to Skype one of your masturbation sessions to everyone you know

OR

one of your bowel movements?

Would you rather...

eat two live baby hamsters

OR

have sex with _____ ?

(insert disgusting acquaintance)

YOU MUST CHOOSE!

Would you rather...

stick your penis in a wasp nest

OR

_____ 's mouth?

(insert disgusting acquaintance)

Would you rather...

give the person to your right a prostate exam

OR

receive one from them?

YOU MUST CHOOSE!

Would you rather...

give a blumpkin to John Madden

OR

have three fingers cut off at the knuckle?

Would you rather...

get a golden shower from various white NBA seven footers

OR

get the shocker from Billy Dee Williams?

Things to consider: "Works every time!"

YOU MUST CHOOSE!

Would you rather...

find a sex video of your best friend and your boyfriend/girlfriend

OR

of your parents?

Would you rather...

gargle with bird shit

OR

_____ ?
(insert disgusting liquid)

YOU MUST CHOOSE!

Would you rather...

dry-hump a giant cheese grater naked

OR

a fan with the safety plate off?

Would you rather...

suck the venom from a snake bite from your best friend's inner thigh

OR

get peed on by your friend to help with a jellyfish sting?

YOU MUST CHOOSE!

If your life depended on it, would you rather...

defecate on the hood of a parked cop car

OR

on your girlfriend/boyfriend's chest?

Would you rather...

find out the tuna salad you just ate was made with semen

OR

that the special sauce on your burger was bile mixed with blood?

YOU MUST CHOOSE!

Would you rather...

be stuck on a deserted island with hungry cannibals *OR* horny prisoners?

flesh-eating giant rodents *OR* your parents and in-laws?

a doppleganger of yourself *OR* a sexually open-minded robot?

Would you rather...

give a hand job to a gorilla

OR

receive one from a gorilla? A koala? A CPA?

YOU MUST CHOOSE!

In a pinch, would you rather...

masturbate into a potted plant

OR

your roommate's sock?

Would you rather...

thread barbed wire up your urethra

OR

eat, digest, and excrete a throwing star?

YOU MUST CHOOSE!

If your lover begged you to administer a Dirty Sanchez, would you rather do it or not?

Dutch oven?

Dog in the bath tub?

Glassbottom boat?

The Neopolitan—excreting, ejaculating, and creating a bruise all in three neat columns?

Note: This page excerpted from the *Bhagavad Gita*, translated from the original Sanskrit.

YOU MUST CHOOSE!

Would you rather...

take a deep sniff of cayenne pepper *OR* the BOMB of the nearest male to you?

get sacked by Shawne Merriman *OR* "sacked" by Shawne Merriman?

star in a porno *OR* in a Robin Williams movie?

Things to consider: Which is more shameful?

YOU MUST CHOOSE!

Would you rather...

have your temperature measured anally

OR

orally with an unwashed anal thermometer?

Would you rather...

get molested by Bigfoot

OR

Toucan Sam?

YOU MUST CHOOSE!

Would you rather watch a stripper...

who was 80-years-old *OR* who weighed 400 pounds?

who keeps farting *OR* who looks a little like your mom?

who dances '80s breakdancing *OR* does a *Stomp* routine?

YOU MUST CHOOSE!

Would you rather...

play strip poker with the cast of *The View*

OR

60 Minutes?

Would you rather...

delicately place your penis in the mouth of a cow

OR

in a French fry fryer?

YOU MUST CHOOSE!

CHAPTER SIX

Would you...

"Everybody has a price... for the million dollar man."
—D.H. Lawrence

Tired of having to read three words before getting to the meat of a question? Well, you're in luck. It's down to two. These "Would you..." questions will show you what you're really made of, what you're willing to do for money or sex, and whether you're willing to make selfless sacrifices. Think you are a good person? Let's find out.

Would you... have sex with Susan Boyle to have sex with Carrie Underwood?

Would you... lick peanut butter off a dog's balls to save an endangered animal species?

Would you... get one DD breast implant for $900,000?

YOU MUST CHOOSE!

Would you... lose half an inch of girth to gain two inches of length? (women: "have your partner...")

Would you... berate an old woman for no reason for fifteen minutes in order to titty-fuck Jessica Alba? (women: receive oral from Johnny Depp)

Would you... slice off a nipple and quickly eat it for $250,000?

YOU MUST CHOOSE!

Would you... slyly masturbate to completion on a public bus for $10,000? At your office desk for $15,000? In a Radio Shack for $18,000? During a haircut for $35,000? At a funeral for $50,000?

YOU MUST CHOOSE!

Would you... give up sex for monk-like wisdom and calm of mind?

Would you... never have sex again for world peace?

Would you... punch a rabbi in the nose in order to get a BJ from Taylor Swift?

YOU MUST CHOOSE!

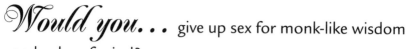

Would you... dial 911 and attempt phone sex for $10,000?

Would you... dial 411 and ask the operator what he or she is currently wearing for $20? Prove it.

Would you... be willing to make out with the same sex if a dramatic role in a movie required it? Who would you pick of your friends to star opposite of you if you had to pick?

YOU MUST CHOOSE!

Would you . . . allow your wife or husband to make out with and messily grope a stranger one time in order to lower your mortgage interest rate by 1%?

Would you . . . French kiss your pet for $100? Prove it.

Would you . . . attend a full season's games of the nearest WNBA team for a threesome with Erin Andrews and Anna Kournikova?

YOU MUST CHOOSE!

Would you... sleep with the ugliest person at school/work (with no repercussions) for a promotion?

Would you... watch your parents have sex thrice to end world hunger?

YOU MUST CHOOSE!

Would you... screw Megan Fox/Brad Pitt if you knew a random person in the world would die because of it?

Would you... hunt and kill 50 pandas with a bow and arrow to be able to have sex whenever and with whomever you choose?

Would you... (men) engage in heavy petting with Zac Efron in order to ensure there are no more *High School Musical* movies ever made again?

YOU MUST CHOOSE!

Would you... screw Amy Winehouse in order to have her become sober and healthy?

Would you... suckle from a nursing cow to suckle from Scarlett Johansson?

Would you... shoot seltzer water into the face of a homeless person in order to sleep with your choice of Taylor Lautner/Alyssa Milano?

YOU MUST CHOOSE!

No one likes it when actors and actresses get mixed up in politics. Nonetheless, which of the following would you do?

Would you... have sex with Hillary Clinton to get to have sex with your choice of Hilary Swank or Hilary Duff?

Former Mexican President Vicente Fox to get to have sex with Megan Fox?

Late Senator Strom Thurmond for Uma Thurman?

Jesse Jackson for Janet Jackson?

Michael Moore for your choice of Mandy or Demi Moore?

YOU MUST CHOOSE!

For the Guys

Would you... have your favorite sports team win every game they played, as long as it was always preceded by you being bukkaked on by 20 Asian businessmen? What would your team's record be if this were the case? When would you step in?

Would you... toss the salad of your offensive linemen to be quarterback for a game in the NFL?

Would you... try to continue having sex with a very hot drunk woman if she threw up a little during sex? What would you say?

YOU MUST CHOOSE!

For the Ladies

Would you... screw Hugh Jackman if it gave you shingles?

Would you... shave Alan Alda's balls for $500 a ball?

Would you... date Mike Tyson for $1,000 a day? How many days would you last?

YOU MUST CHOOSE!

Would you... wreck your car to nail Adriana Lima? What if she was 5 months pregnant? 9 months?

Would you... have a three-way with Optimus Prime and Megatron to peacefully resolve the long-standing war between Decepticons and Autobots?

Would you... want to date a creature who was half person/half couch?

YOU MUST CHOOSE!

Would you. . . post a Youtube video of you crapping in order to have sex with a Victoria's Secret model?

Would you. . . give a handjob to your choice of Joe Perry or William Perry to get a blowjob from Katy Perry?

Would you. . . do Tyler Perry in drag for 1/100th of his wealth?

YOU MUST CHOOSE!

Would you. . . become a vegan for a year for a threesome with Natalie Portman and Zooey Deschanel?

Would you. . . give your left nut for all the tea in China?

Would you. . . miss a year of life with your partner in order to relive your senior year of college?

YOU MUST CHOOSE!

To have sex with anyone of your choice, would you...

consume a bottle of mayonnaise in ten minutes?

poop in your pants for a week?

increase global warming by 1 degree immediately?

YOU MUST CHOOSE!

To have sex with your celebrity crush, would you...

eat 15 bull testicles?

not wear deodorant for a year?

get a genital piercing that has your keys attached to it?

change your legal name permanently to "Prelnar"?

sneak up behind your mom, and knock her legs out from under her?

YOU MUST CHOOSE!

Would you... dive down a urine-soaked Slip-n-Slide to have unlimited breast play with Jennifer Love Hewitt?

Would you... receive an anal pile-driver from John Goodman in order to give six underprivileged inner city youths a full scholarship to the college of their choice?

Would you... appear as a contestant on a Japanese game show called "Happy Good Time Crotch Destroy Show" for a chance to win 10,000,000 Yen?

YOU MUST CHOOSE!

Would you... receive a pearl necklace from Louie Anderson if it turned into a real high quality pearl necklace? If this continued to happen, how many times would you engage?

Would you... administer reciprocal blumpkins with World Wrestling Entertainment's Mark Henry for two million dollars?

YOU MUST CHOOSE!

Would you. . . spend a weekend having sex with Eva Mendes, if you had a 49% chance of catching genital warts? HIV? An STD that caused your groin to smoke when exposed to sunlight?

Would you. . . have sex with Carrie Fisher now to be able to relive time and have sex with Carrie Fisher when you were 15 and she was in *Return of the Jedi*?

YOU MUST CHOOSE!

CHAPTER SEVEN

Who'd You Rather...?
Part 2: Electric Boogaloo

Still looking for that perfect somebody? The yin to your sexual yang? Well, your yang need not be alone much longer. Luckily there are plenty more people, robots, mascots, cartoons, and inanimate objects to sift through. So keep plugging away until you find Mr. or Mrs. Right (or at least Mr. or Mrs. Right Angle!) Wait, no... that's not how it goes.

Would you rather have sex with...

a die-hard liberal who's conservative in bed

OR

a die-hard conservative who's liberal in bed? Who'd you rather marry?

Would you rather...

bang the office hottie on your boss's desk

OR

your high school crush in the principal's office?

YOU MUST CHOOSE!

Would you rather have sex with...

Steve Carell *OR* Stephen Colbert?

Derek Jeter *OR* Kobe Bryant?

Joel McHale *OR* Robert Downey, Jr.?

Tom Colicchio *OR* Simon Cowell?

The Manning brothers *OR* the Jonas Brothers?

Pat Sajak *OR* Alex Trebek?

YOU MUST CHOOSE!

Would you rather have sex with...

Kristin Kreuk *OR* Brooke Burke?

Marisa Miller *OR* Adriana Lima?

Sharon Stone in her prime *OR* Kathy Ireland in her prime?

Minka Kelly *OR* Minka the porn star (world's largest-breasted Asian)?

Pelbin Frolkdarp *OR* Lelsgahn Nasklope? (Go with your instinct.)

YOU MUST CHOOSE!

Would you rather...

bang the *Sex in the City* characters in increasing order of sluttiness

OR

your choice of two panelists on *The View*?

Would you rather have sex with...

Lady Gaga

OR

with a few of her stage outfits?

YOU MUST CHOOSE!

Would you rather have sex with...

Sam Worthington's paraplegic marine character in *Avatar* *OR* his blue alien avatar?

Prince Harry *OR* Prince William?

Mr. Rogers *OR* Captain Kangaroo?

Adam Lambert *OR* Ruben Studdard?

YOU MUST CHOOSE!

Which threesome partners would you rather have?

former couple Padma Lakshmi and Salman Rushdie *OR* Woody Allen and Soon Yi?

Jerry Lewis and Juliette Lewis *OR* Cameron Diaz and Camryn Manheim?

Sienna Miller and Dennis Miller *OR* Halle Berry and Franken Berry?

YOU MUST CHOOSE!

Would you rather have sex with...

this guy

OR
this guy?

YOU MUST CHOOSE!

Would you rather have sex with...

Abe Lincoln

OR

George Washington?

Would you rather have sex with...

The Lord of the Ring's Gandalf

OR

Frodo Baggins?

Things to consider: fireball spell, Gandalf's staff, hobbits' penchant for buggery

YOU MUST CHOOSE!

Would you rather...

attend an orgy with *The Real Housewives of Orange County*

OR

The Real Housewives of New Jersey?

Would you rather have sex with...

Ashley Olsen if she lost 50 pounds

OR

Kirstie Alley if she gained 50 pounds?

YOU MUST CHOOSE!

The Natural World

Would you rather have sex with...

a koala that has been given PCP *OR* a wolverine that has been given Ecstasy?

a shy pelican *OR* a randy baby giraffe?

a manatee in a Jacuzzi *OR* a penguin in a gravity-free chamber?

YOU MUST CHOOSE!

Mashups!

Which of the following hybrids (a being that is a mix of two people) would you rather have sex with?

Kirk Cameron Diaz *OR* Tera Patrick Dempsey?

Rachael Ray Lewis *OR* Liv Tyler Perry?

Robert Blake Lively *OR* Nate Hayden Panettiere?

YOU MUST CHOOSE!

Would you rather...

be slapped by an ugly girl

OR

thrown up on by a hot girl?

Would you rather have sex with...

everyone who has ever held a Guinness World Record for a physical oddity or deformity

OR

all of the people who have ever appeared as a guest on the *Jerry Springer Show*?

Things to consider: fat twins on motorcycles, long nails dude, world's most rotund knees guy

YOU MUST CHOOSE!

Would you rather have sex with...

a half-sized Charlie Sheen

OR

a double-sized Mr. T?

Would you rather have sex with...

Jessica Biel but get crabs

OR

make out with Meredith Vieira and get a free Big Gulp?

YOU MUST CHOOSE!

Would you rather have sex with...

Johnny 5 (the robot from *Short Circuit*)

OR

Robocop?

Would you rather have sex with...

The Quaker Oats mascot in a bed of his oatmeal

OR

Uncle Ben in a bed of his rice?

Things to consider: Both will be done in under 5 minutes.

YOU MUST CHOOSE!

Would you rather have sex with…

Emeril Lagasse and then have him cook a four course meal for you

OR

Christian Bale and then have him chew you out for not getting something right?

Would you rather have sex with…

a purple Rush Limbaugh

OR

a Caucasian Grimace?

YOU MUST CHOOSE!

Would you rather...

give an Arabian Goggles to Hamid Karzai

OR

give a Rusty Trombone to Vladimir Putin?

Would you rather...

give a Shocker to Supreme Court Justice Ruth Bader Ginsburg

OR

"Space Dock" 89-year-old White House reporter Helen Thomas?

Things to consider: Here are some random terms. See if you can make up what the sex act would consist of: Ice Cream Sandwich; Frankenstein; a North Dakota Prairie Dog; a BLT

YOU MUST CHOOSE!

Nerds Only

Would you rather...

have group sex with Queen Amidala, Yoda, and R2D2 from *Star Wars*

OR

Lee Adama, Six, and one of the metallic cylons from *Battlestar Galactica*?

Would you rather...

have a threeway with *Star Trek*'s Seven of Nine and the entire Borg

OR

Erin Grey as Wilma on *Buck Rogers* and Twiki?

Things to consider: Twiki's head is a circumcised penis

YOU MUST CHOOSE!

Would you rather have sex with...

Carmen Electra with skin as sticky as duct tape

OR

Jennifer Garner with funhouse mirror proportions?

Would you rather have sex with...

Representative Barney Frank

OR

Barney the Purple Dinosaur?

Things to consider: Both are gay

YOU MUST CHOOSE!

Would you rather have sex with...

Grace Park *OR* Mila Kunis?

Jenna Jameson *OR* Tila Tequila?

Elizabeth Berkley *OR* Elisabeth Hasselbeck?

Tiffani-Amber Thiessen *OR* Tiffani Thiessen?

YOU MUST CHOOSE!

Would you rather...

have a gangbang with an NFL team after they've just won the Super Bowl

OR

after they've just lost the Super Bowl?

Would you rather have sex with...

Santa and Mrs. Claus

OR

the Tooth Fairy and the Easter Bunny?

YOU MUST CHOOSE!

Deal or No Deal Revisited

Deal Host Howie Mandel also hosts the *Would You Rather...?*
DVD game, available now at retailers and published
by Imagination Games. Here then are some questions
combining both games.

Would you rather...

have a chance for the one million dollars

OR

a chance to have sex with all of the models holding the
briefcases?

YOU MUST CHOOSE!

Would you rather...

take the deal of $20,000

OR

sex with one of the models?

Would you rather...

play the game for cash

OR

play the game where instead, each $10,000 = one model you get to have sex with? So you could take one woman or take the chance and go for more. However, there are also other things to have sex with as revealed inside the briefcase: cast of the *Biggest Loser*, livestock, NBA seven footers, cast of the *Biggest Luger*, etc. Does this make sense? I'm hungry. The Banker would be The Pimp.

YOU MUST CHOOSE!

Would you rather have sex with...

Kristen Stewart from *Twilight* **OR** Anna Paquin from *True Blood*?

Jorja Fox on the set of *CSI* **OR** one of the models on the set of the *Price is Right*?

a woman with no hair **OR** a woman with a soul patch?

the cast of *Jersey Shore* **OR** the creatures in Jabba the Hutt's fortress?

a Honda Civic **OR** a Chrysler LeBaron?

YOU MUST CHOOSE!

Would you rather have sex with...

a mustached Johnny Depp *OR* clean-shaven Johnny Depp?

Alan Greenspan with a 12-inch schlong *OR* Tom Brady with a one-incher?

Keith Richards *OR* a fresh corpse?

a narcoleptic Munchkin *OR* a bulimic Oompa Loompa?

YOU MUST CHOOSE!

Would you rather...

give head to Cinderella *OR* get head from her ugly stepsisters?

get a snowball from John Madden *OR* assume his physique?

toss Gary Busey's salad *OR* have his brain for a month?

YOU MUST CHOOSE!

Would you rather have sex with...

your office's IT department

OR

the janitorial staff?

Would you rather have sex with...

your girlfriend

OR

with Angelina Jolie a second after Brad Pitt came inside her?

YOU MUST CHOOSE!

Would you rather...

have sex with Kelly Osbourne *OR* get a Golden Shower from Kelly Ripa?

Dutch oven the Pope *OR* motorboat Mother Teresa? (Assuming you can go back in time.)

have sex with Kristen Bell with bloody stumps for limbs *OR* Fergie with cloven hooves?

YOU MUST CHOOSE!

Would you rather...

be the meat in a Cagney and Lacey sandwich (with today's Tyne Daly and Sharon Gless)

OR

have armpit sex with Aretha Franklin?

Would you rather have sex with...

a Russian female shot-putter

OR

an exotic evil Russian spy who may or may not try to kill you?

YOU MUST CHOOSE!

Would you rather have phone sex with...

Rosie Perez *OR* Paula Abdul?

Rihanna with a vocoder *OR* Kate Winslet?

Céline Dion in French *OR* Jenna Jameson in Yiddish?

Terry Bradshaw *OR* Shannon Sharpe?

YOU MUST CHOOSE!

Would you rather have phone sex with...

Arnold Schwarzenegger *OR* Kanye West on vocoder

Russell Crowe *OR* the Dwayne "The Rock" Johnson?

Chewbacca *OR* Darth Vader?

someone who has the voice of an effeminate Morgan Freeman *OR* Tom Cruise but he's on speaker phone and there's like a lot of background noise and stuff and it's annoying?

Penn *OR* Teller?

YOU MUST CHOOSE!

Would you rather...

bang the Spice Girls in alphabetical order **OR** in reverse alphabetical order?

see Bill Clinton naked **OR** Hillary?

squeeze your grandmother's ass **OR** your grandfather's ass?

YOU MUST CHOOSE!

Would you rather have sex with...

the cast of the new *90210* **OR** the old *90210*?

Friday Night Lights **OR** *Gossip Girl*?

Smallville **OR** *Ugly Betty*?

the judges of *American Idol* **OR** the judges of *Dancing with the Stars*? What if you would then be judged?

YOU MUST CHOOSE!

CHAPTER EIGHT

Random Play

Welcome to *Would You Rather...?*'s sloppy seconds: the rejects, the neglects, the dirty dregs that deal with sex. Of course, sometimes leftovers taste better than the hot meal... if y'know what we mean! And if you do, please email the answer to leftoversmetaphor@sevenfooter.com, because we have no idea.

Would you rather...

age a year every time you orgasm

OR

only be able to have an orgasm once a year?

Would you rather...

buy a vibrator at a garage sale *OR* from Andy Dick?

used, on eBay, from someone with medium positive feedback *OR* as a hand-me-down from your older sister?

subscribe to Netdix, a Netflix of vibrator/dildos *OR* Netshitz, a Netflix for toilet paper?

YOU MUST CHOOSE!

Would you rather live in a world where...

the average penis length is 2 inches *OR* 20 inches?

where the average breast size is A *OR* HHH?

where if you got hit in the balls, it doesn't hurt, rather they simply fall off and a new pair grows *OR* where ejaculate is lighter than air?

YOU MUST CHOOSE!

Would you rather live in a world where...

when you orgasm, you see God *OR* a delicious ham sandwich appears next to you?

where every time you had sex, you gained a pound *OR* every time you received oral sex, you gained five pounds?

YOU MUST CHOOSE!

Would you rather your only pick-up line be...

"Chinese, Japanese, dirty knees, look at these!" (with accompanying gestures and faces) *OR* "Can I bang you in your bunghole so my sperms don't go up your fallopians?"

"You make me feel like I need to take a sissy!" *OR* "You look like a young Bert Convy."?

YOU MUST CHOOSE!

While you're having sex, would you rather your partner scream out...

"Make love to me." *OR* "Fuck my brains out!!!"?

"Have you ever done this before?" *OR* "Call me Apache Chief!"?

a lukewarm "Fuck that pussy" *OR* a rousing "Fuck that ear!"?

"Treat me like a whore!" *OR* "Kibbles and Bits! Kibbles and Bits! I've got to get me some Kibbles and Bits!"?

YOU MUST CHOOSE!

While you're having sex, would you rather your partner scream out...

"I love you." *OR* "Stick your fingers up my ass, now!"?

"I have gonorrhea." *OR* "That wasn't me having sex, but rather Jesus having sex through me."?

"Put your pee pee in my bagina." *OR* the theme from the animated movie *The Hobbit*?

YOU MUST CHOOSE!

Would you rather...? for beginners?

 Would you rather...

have sex with a hideous person and get herpes

OR

have sex with a superhot person and get a bar of gold?

 Would you rather...

orgasm every time you defecate

OR

defecate every time you orgasm?

YOU MUST CHOOSE!

Wedding Party!

Would you rather...

let your wedding party bang your spouse on the night of your wedding

OR

not be able to consummate your relations with your spouse for five years?

Would you... let your side of the wedding party bang your spouse if you got to bang your spouse's side?

YOU MUST CHOOSE!

Typo Questions:
Because mistakes can be sacred.

Would you rather...

have oral sex *OR* aural sex?

anal sex *OR* banal sex?

a threesome *OR* a treesome?

Would you rather...

have sex wearing a bagel cock ring

OR

through crotchless bologna underwear?

YOU MUST CHOOSE!

Would you rather live in a world where...

everyone's sexual performance is open for reviews on Yelp.com *OR* where you are legally required to have sex with someone if they have collected at least 5000 signatures through an online petition?

every orgasm was accompanied by the Kool-Aid man busting through the wall exclaiming "Oh Yeah!" *OR* where every orgasm killed a member of an endangered species?

Things to consider: Multiple orgasms very destructive or very evil.

YOU MUST CHOOSE!

Would you rather have sex with...

Elizabeth Banks *OR* Rachel McAdams?

Naomi Watts *OR* Anna Faris?

Emmanuelle Chriqui if she was wearing Rec Specs *OR* Keeley Hazell if she was wearing gag glasses with a moustache?

Denise Milani if she were completely flat-chested and had a dumpy ass *OR* Angela Lansbury if she were a 36DD-22-34?

YOU MUST CHOOSE!

Would you rather have sex with...

Clint Eastwood *OR* Michael Cera?

Kanye West *OR* Conan O'Brien?

a good-looking frat guy asshole *OR* a nice but unassertive guy?

a poet *OR* a carpenter?

Jason Bateman if he had Shaq's physique *OR* vice-versa?

YOU MUST CHOOSE!

Would you rather...

let Kimbo Slice have his way with you sexually

OR

fight him?

Would you rather...

have a pet parakeet that repeatedly says "The black man is using the Jew as his muscle to enslave the white race"

OR

have the family dog talk dirty to you while he's licking

his genitals?

YOU MUST CHOOSE!

God-awful Questions

It seems there is some confusion that our book is meant for church youth groups. Keeping that in mind, here are questions of biblical proportions.

Would you rather...

covet thy neighbor's ox *OR* give your virgin daughter away for a dowry of 10 sheep?

Things to consider: the ox-coveting is punishable by stoning to death according to Scripture

sleep with an animal *OR* curse your parents?

Things to consider: Both are punishable by death.

take the Bible literally *OR* anally?

Things to consider: We are going to Hell. What if it's a pocket Bible?

YOU MUST CHOOSE!

Would you rather...

have all your dirty talk in Iambic Pentameter

OR

Haiku?

To YOU / I HAVE / a QUES- / tion I / must ASK /

For YOU / to STICK / your PE- / nis IN / my ASS /

BeFORE / you GO / and GET / your COCK / too
HARD /

I'm GOING / to NEED / to GET / your CRED- / it
CARD /

Fuck that pussy like

willow twig bends in river

night sky falls. Tittay!

YOU MUST CHOOSE!

Classy People Questions

Would you rather...

have sex to Pachelbel's *Canon in D* *OR* Beethoven's 9th Symphony?

get in the mood buy sipping 1973 Brunello Montepulciano *OR* dining by candlelight on Beluga caviar and champagne?

dry-hump a bag of mulch *OR* inappropriately grope an armadillo?

YOU MUST CHOOSE!

Would you rather...

magically experience physical pleasure any time your parents have sex

OR

vice versa?

Would you rather...

have one clean shot to the face of Carson Daly

OR

Ryan Seacrest?

YOU MUST CHOOSE!

Would you rather...

have a scoresheet where you and your partner score each other after each sexual encounter

OR

have an agreement where you and your partner can use yellow/red cards when there is an "infraction" during sex (yellow is a warning, red, you're ejected)?

Would you rather...

have your balls sucked by a dozen leeches

OR

by Rosie O'Donnell?

YOU MUST CHOOSE!

Would You Lather...?

What began as a Japanese man's mispronunciation became an idea unto itself.

Would you lather... a seal?

Would you lather... Al Roker?

Would you lather... your naked body in streaming video on the Internet for $50,000?

YOU MUST CHOOSE!

Would you rather live in a world where...

men and women had electrical plugs and sockets as genitalia *OR* where people had their genitals located on their palms?

Things to consider: Needing an adapter for sex overseas. Clapping or shaking hands.

once a year a siren randomly goes off and you are required to give a rusty trombone to the person standing nearest to you *OR* where regardless of where you went to sleep, every morning you always wake up naked and spooning a complete stranger?

YOU MUST CHOOSE!

Mixed Blessings

Would you rather...

get a million dollars cash and have your penis shortened by three inches *OR* pay $100,000 and get your penis lengthened by one inch?

lose one year off your life to have sex with Carmen Electra *OR* gain one year on your life by having sex with Madeleine Albright?

have the power of flight but only while naked *OR* have the power of invisibility but only as long as you can maintain an erection?

Things to consider: scrotal windburn, suddenly appearing in an embarrassing way

YOU MUST CHOOSE!

Would you rather...

participate in a no-holds barred orgy with the cast of *Lost* *OR* *Gilligan's Island*?

the cast of *Celebrity Rehab* *OR* *Rock of Love*?

the characters in *Heroes* *OR* all the various *Star Trek* incarnations?

Would you rather...

have sex missionary position with a Pole

OR

sex with a missionary playing Pole Position? (work in progress)

YOU MUST CHOOSE!

Would you rather...

find every single person you see unbelievably sexually attractive

OR

find only one in ten thousand people even remotely attractive?

Would you rather...

have the ability to shift which testicle hangs lower than the other by snapping your fingers

OR

have fluorescent orange pee?

Things to consider: party tricks, convincing primitive cultures you are a god

YOU MUST CHOOSE!

(Guys)

Would you rather...

marry someone with a witty mind

OR

who can expertly deep-throat?

(Women)

Would you rather...

marry someone with a stable income

OR

a desire and talent for giving oral sex?

YOU MUST CHOOSE!

Would you rather...

have J.Lo's booty

OR

Salma Hayek's rack?

Would you... perform fellatio on former NBA great Wes Unseld for $5,000? $50,000? How about if it was near the end of his rookie-of-the-year season when he averaged 18.2 rebounds per game?

YOU MUST CHOOSE!

Would you rather...

automatically send out a Twitter update to all your friends every time you masturbate

OR

only be able to masturbate to twitter tweets?

Would you rather...

as a psychic, be able to tell the future from semen stains

OR

pubic hair curl patterns?

Things to consider: Idea for TV show: *The Psychic Prostitute*, sell to Fox, writes itself

YOU MUST CHOOSE!

Would you rather...

have to have sex in a Snuggie

OR

a three-cornered hat and buckled shoes?

Would you rather...

have phone sex with Elmer Fudd

OR

Snagglepuss?

YOU MUST CHOOSE!

Would you rather...

receive $100,000

OR

find out just once what it felt like to have sex as someone of the opposite gender?

Would you rather...

have a Jar Jar Binks speech impediment when hitting on someone

OR

frequently fart the *24* ticking clock sound?

YOU MUST CHOOSE!

Would you rather...

have sex in front of overzealous screaming hockey fans

OR

hushed and politely clapping golf fans, complete with whispered commentary?

Things to consider: "Ooh... looks like he missed the hole. Not sure if he's going to be able to come back from that one... Looking a little flaccid today if you ask me."

Would you... receive and sport corporate-logo-shaped hickeys for $5,000/year? $25,000?

YOU MUST CHOOSE!

Would you rather...

have sex with the hybrid: Pamela Anderson Cooper

OR

Meg Ryan Reynolds?

Would you rather...

have a detachable penis

OR

a penis that vibrates on command?

YOU MUST CHOOSE!

Appendix:

Real Editorial Notes Used During Writing This Book

38 – cut "a" before "your penis"

38 – need quote after "vagina"

60 – add "facials" after "crusting"

65 – cut "?" after defecate

65 – capitalize Constantly Expanding Testicles

81 – cut "of your cock" after "rhinoceros horn on the tip"

82 – add "have" before "a vagina that shoots…"

91 – add "on" before "your taint"

103 – add "get" before "nose-fucked"

131 – change first options of bottom question as follows: have an elastic scrotum that can be used as a nunchucks-like weapon to fight crime

149 ' in question about dropping load in mouth, "Grandma" should lower case –

150 – "nipple side off" should be "nipple slide off"

160 – be fisted by a Edward Scissorhands should be "fisted by Edward Scissorhands"

173 put a comma between "interview" and "hanging brain"

177 – in the anal insertion question, replace TV remote with harmonica;

178 – the top questions second option should just read "one of your bowel movements" not "have sex with one of your bowel movements"

249 – put comma after "balls"

250 - put comma after "sex"; put comma after "BJ"

253 – period after "gonorrhea."

Would You Rather...?:
Love & Sex asks you to
ponder such questions as:

- *Would you rather...* orgasm once every ten years *OR* once every ten seconds?

- *Would you rather...* have to have sex in the same position every night *OR* have to have sex in a different position every night (you can never repeat)?

- *Would you rather...* have breast implants made of Nerf® *OR* Play-Doh®?

- *Would you rather...* vicariously experience all orgasms that occur in your zip code *OR* during sex, have the Microsoft paper clip help icon appear with sex tips?

Would You Rather...?: Love & Sex can be read alone or played together as a game. Laugh-out-loud funny, uniquely imaginative, and deceptively thought-provoking, *Would You Rather...?: Love & Sex* is simultaneously the authors' most mature and immature work yet!

www.sevenfooterpress.com